Wolfgang Amadeus Mozart

THE MARRIAGE OF FIGARO
(Le Nozze di Figaro)

in Full Score

Dover Publications, Inc.
New York

This Dover edition, first published in 1979, is an unabridged republication of the edition by Georg Schünemann and Kurt Soldan, with German translation of the vocal text by Georg Schünemann, originally published by C. F. Peters, Leipzig, n.d. (publication number 11462; editorial matter dated "Summer 1941"). In the present edition all the preliminary matter and the Editors' Commentary (Revisionsbericht), originally in German, appear in a new English translation specially prepared by Stanley Appelbaum.

International Standard Book Number: 0-486-23751-6
Library of Congress Catalog Card Number: 78-67726

Manufactured in the United States of America
Dover Publications, Inc.
31 East 2nd Street
Mineola, N.Y. 11501

THE MARRIAGE OF FIGARO

"DRAMMA GIOCOSO" IN FOUR ACTS
TEXT BY LORENZO DA PONTE
MUSIC BY W. A. MOZART

CHARACTERS

COUNT ALMAVIVA.....................*Baritone*
COUNTESS ALMAVIVA..................*Soprano*
SUSANNA,............................*Soprano*
    her chambermaid, betrothed to
FIGARO, the Count's valet...................*Bass*
CHERUBINO, the Count's page.............*Soprano*
MARCELLINA.....................*Mezzo soprano*
BASILIO, a music teacher....................*Tenor*
DON CURZIO, a judge.......................*Tenor*
BARTOLO, a doctor in Seville.................*Bass*
ANTONIO, the Count's gardener and
    uncle of Susanna...................*Bass*
BARBARINA, his daughter.................*Soprano*

Peasant men and women. Guests. Huntsmen.
House servants.

The action takes place at the château
of Count Almaviva.

DRAMMA GIOCOSO IN QUATTRO ATTI
POESIA DI LORENZO DA PONTE
MUSICA DI W. A. MOZART

PERSONAGGI

IL CONTE DI ALMAVIVA................*Baritono*
LA CONTESSA DI ALMAVIVA............*Soprano*
SUSANNA,............................*Soprano*
    sua Cameriera e promessa sposa di
FIGARO, Cameriere del Conte................*Basso*
CHERUBINO, Paggio del Conte.............*Soprano*
MARCELLINA.....................*Mezzosoprano*
BASILIO, Maestro di musica.................*Tenore*
DON CURZIO, Giudice......................*Tenore*
BARTOLO, Medico di Siviglia................*Basso*
ANTONIO, Giardiniere del Conte e Zio
    di Susanna........................*Basso*
BARBARINA, sua figlia..................*Soprano*

Contadini e Contadine. Convitati. Cacciatori.
Servitori.
La scena si finge nel castello del Conte
di Almaviva.

Composed in 1785/6. First performed at the National Court Theater
in Vienna on May 1, 1786, under the composer's direction.

INSTRUMENTATION

2 Flutes (Flauti) - 2 Oboes (Oboi) - 2 Clarinets (Clarinetti) - 2 Bassoons (Fagotti) - 2 Horns (Corni)
2 Trumpets (Trombe) - 2 Kettledrums (Timpani) - Violins (Violini) I & II - Violas (Viole)
Cellos (Violoncelli) - Basses (Contrabassi)

CONTENTS

PREFACE

In the National Court Theater in Vienna on May 1, 1786, a new opera by Wolfgang Amadeus Mozart received its first performance: *Le Nozze di Figaro* (The Marriage of Figaro).

The playbill of the world premiere reads:

Oggi (1. maggio 1786) per la prima volta

LE NOZZE DI FIGARO

ossia la folle giornata

Dramma giocoso in quattro atti. Parole del Sign. Abbate da Ponte, musica del Sign. Amadeo Mozart.

Personaggi:

Il conte di Almaviva	Sign. Mandini
La Contessa di Almaviva	Signora Laschi
Susanna, sua cameriera	Signora Storace
e promessa sposa di	
Figaro, cameriere del Conte	Sign. Benucci
Cherubino, paggio del Conte	Signora Bussani
Marcellina	Signora Mandini
Basilio, maestro di musica	
Don Curzio, giudice	Sign. Occhelly [Kelly]
Bartolo, medico di Seviglia	Sign. Bussani
Antonio, giardiniere del Conte e zio	
di Susanna	Sign. Bussani
Barberina, sua figlia	Signora Nanina Gottlieb

Contadini e contadine. - Convitati, cacciatori. - Servitori.
La scena si finge nel castello del conte di Almaviva.

Mozart, in a joyful burst of creativity, had completed the opera in barely half a year, while also working on three new piano concertos (E-flat Major, A Major and C Minor), a violin sonata, *Der Schauspieldirektor* and other projects. The libretto offered him a subject after his own heart. Here he found a comedy based on living actuality by Beaumarchais *(Le Mariage de Figaro, ou La folle journée)*, which had successfully triumphed over adverse parties and opinions; above all, it contained musically grateful situations and climaxes. Lorenzo da Ponte, an experienced librettist who had turned his hand to all sorts of texts for music, had to revise and simplify his model and free it of all tendentiousness and applications to the current moment. As for all his operas, Mozart made decisive contributions to the shaping of the text, now making an addition, now supplying new ideas and suggestions based on the spirit of the music. In this way the time-honored machinery of opera buffa—disguise, mistaken identity and intrigue—were freed of all routine elements and subordinated to a swiftly moving, lively interplay of passions and errors. Mozart imbued the persons and scenes with the nobility of his musical personality; all incidental and everyday matters have acquired the character of a personal, free statement that goes far beyond the immediate moment. The opera buffa has become a reflection of human foibles and characters seen through the magical glow of Mozart's all-transfiguring melody.

In Germany the opera was soon given with a German text. As early as a year after the world premiere, a German translation was prepared for the Fürstenberg Theater in Donaueschingen. This anonymous, still considerably clumsy version was shortly followed by others for Passau, Frankfurt and Berlin. The interesting Passau translation (1789) contains many felicitous turns of phrase, whereas the Berlin version by Christian August Vulpius (1790) is more successful in the recitatives than in the arias and ensembles. Many passages from it have been retained to the present day. For the Hamburg performance a German version was supplied by Baron von Knigge (1791). This translation, too, furnished many well-chosen words and characteristic phrases. Mozart's own manuscript, which is among the most prized treasures of the Prussian State Library, includes a German translation along with the Italian text. This translation, which was certainly done within the eighteenth century, covers the arias and ensembles but not the recitatives. It includes some verses familiar to all of us: "Will einst das Gräflein ein Tänzchen wagen"; "Nun vergiss"; "Ihr, die ihr Triebe"; "Komm heraus, verworfner Knabe"; "So lang hab' ich geschmachtet"; and others. From this point on, the translations increase in number. K. L. Giesecke's version appeared in 1792, and further texts appeared in 1798, 1814, 1815, 1844, etc., basically following Knigge and Vulpius. In 1847 Eduard Devrient published a translation, as did Kugler in 1857, and then Carl Niese, in the Mozart *Complete Works* edition, set forth his own revision, which did away with earlier errors (1874). In 1880 Schletterer undertook an improvement, and in 1899 Hermann Levi published a reworking of the old sources. The last versions were those of Max Kalbeck in Vienna (1906) and Siegfried Anheisser in Berlin (1931). Both of these aim at a totally new approach: Kalbeck using a free, completely self-standing form; Anheisser doing his best to achieve a literal translation. Most of the older and newer printed vocal scores are based on the above-mentioned German librettos.

If one takes the trouble to work through all these translations, to which others could be added, one is constantly amazed by the wealth of ideas and new and adapted coinages that they contain. The most divergent viewpoints are represented: one translator wants to be as literal as possible; another is more interested in general sense and expression than in individual words; a third wants to capture Mozart's music or the Italian vowels in his text and sacrifices everything to the dramatic continuity. Some translators even venture upon more or less thoroughgoing alterations, depending on the demands of time and place, purpose and goal of the performance.

The new version of the German text in the present volume attempts to point a way out of the confusing multiplicity of all these experiments. It is based on the practical knowledge that German operagoers will not have any philologically exact translations forced on them, no matter how well meant, but continue to prefer the old words and verses of which they have grown fond, as they have been sung for generations and as they are performed in the home. No literal translation, however knowledgeable, can replace the popular favor of the old texts. Therefore in actual performances as well, the custom has developed of retaining the best material from the old translations.

This time-honored tradition forms the basis of the present new version. For the first time the old texts were critically sifted, and the best version of each passage was chosen. Phrase by phrase, word by word, comparisons were made between the still available libretto publications, both German and Italian, and all the older and newer vocal scores and orchestral scores were consulted, in order to investigate every turn of phrase that developed in the course of the centuries. Both text and music were checked against Mozart's own manuscript. In places where the old versions are unsatisfactory, a new translation in the sense and spirit of Mozart's music was made most circumspectly after a careful consideration of all suggestions. In doing so, changes were made in a few passages in accordance with the differently situated German stress in words and phrases, in order not to sound unnatural and affected.

In the editing of the score, the conductor Kurt Soldan helped me immeasurably with his great knowledge and his exactitude in all matters of textual criticism. I would like to express my thanks to him here too.

Berlin, Summer 1941

GEORG SCHÜNEMANN

DIE HOCHZEIT DES FIGARO
LE NOZZE DI FIGARO
Sinfonia

W. A. Mozart
(1756–1791)

4

6

8

18

19

attacca subito
il Duettino di Susanna e Figaro [Nº 1]

ERSTER AKT
[Ein noch nicht vollständig möbliertes Zimmer
mit einem Lehnstuhl in der Mitte.]
Erste Szene
Susanna. Figaro.
[Figaro mit einem Zollstock in der Hand; Susanna setzt sich,
am Spiegel stehend, einen mit Blumen geschmückten Hut auf]

ATTO PRIMO
[Camera non affatto ammobiliata
con una sedia d'appoggio in mezzo.]
Scena I
Susanna e Figaro.
[Figaro con una misura in mano, e Susanna allo specchio
che si sta mettendo un cappellino ornato di fiori]

No. 1. Duettino

Recitativo

attacca subito il Duettino [N⁰ 2]

Nº 2. Duettino

kling, nur zwei Sprün-ge, und du bist bei ihr.
din, in due pas-si da quel-la puoi gir.

Und
Vien

will gar der Graf mir Ge-schäf-te be-stel-len,
poi l'oc-ca-sio-ne che vuol mi il pa-dro-ne,

Ge-schäf-te be-
che vuol mi il pa-

stel-len, husch, husch, husch, husch, in drei Sprün-gen er-reich ich die Tür.
dro-ne, don don, don don, in tre sal-ti lo va-do a ser-vir.

Recitativo

Susanna: Wohl-an denn, so hör und schweige.
Or be - ne; a-scol-ta,e ta - ci.

Figaro [beunruhigt] [inquieto]: Re-de, was gibt es Neu-es?
Par-la, che c è di nuo-vo?

Susanna: Der gnäd'ge Herr ist es nun schon mü - de, nach
Il si-gnor Con-te stan-co di an-dar cac-cian-do le stra-

frem-den Schö - nen zu ja-gen, er will hier in der Nä - he, will im Schloß sein Glück ver-su-chen; doch nicht nach sei-ner
nie-re bel-lez-ze fo-re-stie - re, vuo-le an-cor nel ca-stel-lo ri-ten-tar la sua sor-te; nè già di sua con-

Zweite Szene

[Figaro (allein).]

[Figaro geht lebhaft auf und ab und reibt sich die Hände]

Scena II

[Figaro (solo).]

[Figaro passeggiando con foco per la camera, e fregandosi le mani]

segue la Cavatina di Figaro [Nº 3]

Nº 3. Cavatina

44

lei - se, _____ lei - se, lei - se, lei - se, lei - se, lei - se, lei - er,
pia - no, _____ pia - no, pia - no, pia - no, pia - no, pia - no, pia - no,

nach mei - ner Wei - se von dem Ge - heim - nis den Schlei - er ziehn! Mit fei - nen Knif-fen,
me - glio o - gni ar - ca - no dis - si - mu - lan - do sco - prir po - trò! L'ar - te scher-men-do,

Graf ein Tänzchen nun wa-gen, mag er's mir sa-gen, ich spiel_ihm auf, mag er's mir sa - gen, ich spiel ihm auf, ja,
la - re, si-gnor con-ti - no, il chi-tar-ri-no le suo-ne - rò, il chi-tar - ri - no le suo-ne-rò, sì,

ich spiel ihm auf, ja, ich spiel ihm auf.
le suo-ne - rò, si, le suo-ne - rò.

Dritte Szene
Bartolo. Marcellina (mit einem Kontrakt in der Hand).

Scena III
Bartolo, e Marcellina (con un contratto in mano).

Recitativo

Sie zö-ger-ten so lang bis zum Ta-ge sei-ner Hoch-zeit, sich mit mir zu be - ra-ten? Noch ist es
Ed a-spet-ta-ste il gior-no fis-sa-to a le sue noz-ze per par-lar-mi di que-sto? Io non mi

48

segue l'Aria di Bartolo [Nº 4]

№ 4. Aria

55

Vierte Szene

Marcellina. Dann Susanna
[welche eine Haube, ein Band und ein Damenkleid trägt].

Scena IV

Marcellina, poi Susanna
[con cuffia da donna, un nastro, e un abito da donna].

Recitativo

attacca il Duettino [Nº5]

№ 5. Duettino

65

Fünfte Szene

Susanna. Dann Cherubino.

Scena V

Susanna e poi Cherubino.

Recitativo

68

segue l'Aria di Cherubino [N⁰ 6]

№ 6. Aria

Sechste Szene
Cherubino. Susanna. Dann der Graf.

[Cherubino sieht im Abgehn von weitem den Grafen, kehrt erschrocken um und verbirgt sich hinter dem Sessel]

Scena VI
Cherubino. Susanna, e poi il Conte.

[Cherubino va per partire, e vedendo il Conte da lontano, torna indietro impaurito, e si nasconde dietro la sedia]

Recitativo

78

attacca il Terzetto [Nº 7]

Nº 7. Terzetto

55
Ob.
Clar. in B
Fag.
cresc.
p
Viol. I
Viol. II
Viola
[cresc.]
tr
(Sich dem Sessel nähernd [um sie darauf zu setzen])
(Approssimandosi al sedile [in atto di farla sedere])
Bas.
Herz - chen im Bu - sen pocht!
Di - o, le bat - te il cor!
Still, ich will den Ses - sel ho - len.
Pian pia - nin su que - sto seg - gio.
Gf.
Herz - chen im Bu - sen pocht!
Di - o, le bat - te il cor!
Vc.
Cb.
62
Cor. in B
p cresc.
f
fp
Susanna
S.
Gott, wo bin ich?
Do - ve so - no?
(Erholt sich)
(Rinviene)
Wie, was seh ich?
Co - sa veg - gio!
(Sich von beiden losreißend)
(Staccandosi da tutti due)
Wel - che Kühn - heit, laßt mich los, laßt mich al -
Che in - so - len - za, an - da - te fuor, an - da - te

Recitativo

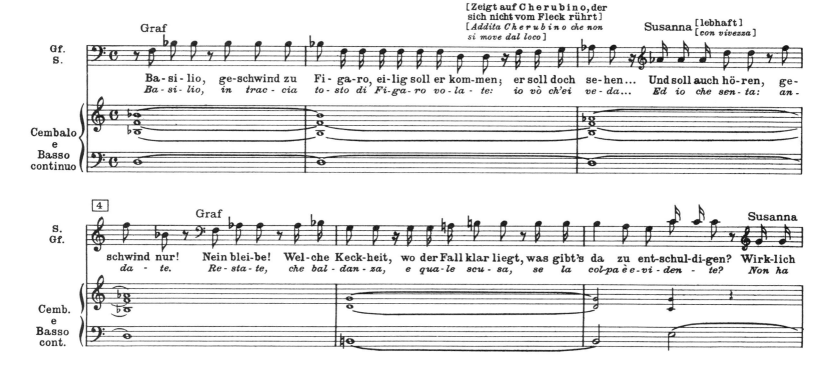

96

Achte Szene

[Figaro. Bauern und Bäuerinnen. Die Vorigen.]

[Figaro trägt ein weißes Kleid in der Hand. Die Bauern, weiß gekleidet, streuen aus kleinen Körben Blumen vor die Füße des Grafen]

Scena VIII

[Figaro, Contadine e Contadini, i suddetti.]

[Figaro con bianca veste in mano. Coro di contadine e di contadini vestiti di bianco, che spargono fiori, raccolti in piccioli panieri, davanti il Conte]

Nº 8. Coro

Recitativo

№ 8a. Coro

Recitativo

segue l'Aria di Figaro [N⁹9]

№ 9. Aria

wän-der. Nun ver-giß lei-ses Flehn, sü-ßes Ko - sen, und das Flat-tern von Ro - se zu Ro-sen; du wirst
lan-te. Non più andrai, far-fal-lo-ne a-mo-ro - so, not-te e gior-no d'in-tor-no gi - ran-do; del-le

nicht mehr die Her-zen er-o-bern, ein A - do - nis, ein klei-ner Nar-ziß, du wirst nicht mehr die Her-zen er-o-bern, ein A-
bel - le turbando il ri-po-so, Nar-ci-set- to, A-don-ci - no d'a-mor, del-le bel - le turbando il ri-po-so, Nar-ci-

Ende des ersten Aktes
Fine dell'Atto primo

ZWEITER AKT
[Ein prächtiges Zimmer mit einem Alkoven
und drei Türen.]

Erste Szene
Die Gräfin (allein).

ATTO SECONDO
[Camera ricca, con alcova,
e tre porte.]

Scena I
La Contessa (sola).

№ 10. Cavatina

attacca subito

Dritte Szene
Die Gräfin. Susanna. Später Cherubino.

Scena III
La Contessa, Susanna, poi Cherubino.

Recitativo

100 Gräfin: Ach, wie pein-lich, Su-san-na, daß die-ser jun-ge Mensch des Gra-fen Ge-spräch mit an - hö-ren muß-te! Ach, du
Quan-to duol-mi, Su-san-na, che que-sto gio-vi-not - to ab-bia del Con - te le stra-va-gan-ze u-di-to! ah tu non

104 weißt nicht... Doch war-um hat denn Cherubin sich an mich nicht ge-wendet? Wo ist die Kan-zo-net-te? Hier ist sie, und gleich, wenn er
sa - i... ma per qual cau-sa ma - i da me stes-sa ei non ven-ne? Dov' è la can-zo-net-ta? Ec-co-la: ap-pun-to fac-

Susanna

108 kommt, soll er sie sin-gen. Stil - le, wer kommt da? Er ist es. Nur nä-her, nä-her, mein ta - pfrer Herr
ciam che ce la can - ti. Zit - to, vien gen-te; è des-so: a-van-ti, a-van-ti, si-gnor uf-fi-zi-

111 Cherubino: Hauptmann. Nen-ne mich nicht mit dem ver-haß-ten Na-men, der mich er - in-nert, daß ich sie mei-den soll, ach, die Pa-tin, die so
a - le. Ah non chia-mar-mi con no-me sì fa-ta-le, ei mi ram-men-ta, che ab-ban-do-nar deggi - o co-ma-re tan-to

115 Susanna: gut ist! Cherubino (seufzend) (sospirando): Und die so schön ist! Ach, ja, so schön! Susanna (spottet ihm nach) (imitandolo): Ach, ja, so schön! Sie klei-ner Heuch-ler, ge-schwind die Kan-zo-
buo-na! E tan-to bel-la! Ah sì... cer-to... Ah sì... cer-to... I-po-cri-to-ne, via pre-sto la can-

119 net-te, die Sie mir heu-te ga-ben, der Frau Grä-fin vor-ge-sun-gen! Gräfin: Wer ist der Dich-ter? Susanna [auf Cherubino zeigend] [additando Cherubino]: O sehn Sie, wie sei-ne
zo-ne, che sta-ma-ne a me de-ste, a ma-da-ma can-ta-te. Chi n'è l'au-tor? Guar-da-te: e-gli ha due

segue l'Arietta di Cherubino [Nº 11]

Nº 11. Arietta

Sagt, hol-de Frau — en, die ihr_ sie_kennt, sagt, ist es
[Ihr, die ihr Trie - be des Her — -zens kennt,]
Voi che sa - pe - te che co - sa è a - mor, don - ne ve-

Lie — be, was hier so brennt, sagt, ist es Lie — be,_ was hier_ so_brennt?
de - te s'io Vho nel cor, don - ne ve - de - te_ s'io Vho_ nel_ cor.

Recitativo

134

segue l'Aria di Susanna [Nº12]

№ 12. Aria

[Während Susanna
[Cherubino, mentre

sach-te, sachte umgedreht,   bra-vo,   so ist es gut;
pia-no or via gi-ra-te-vi: bra-vo,   và ben co-sì,

ihn frisiert, wirft Cherubino der Gräfin zärtliche Blicke zu]
Susanna lo sta acconciando, guarda la Contessa teneramente]

nun wen-den Sie auf mich den Blick,   nicht
la fac-cia o-ra vol-ge-te-mi,   o-

um-ge-wandt,   mich an-geschaut,   bra-vo,
ra - te - vi...   *guar - da - te - mi...*   *bra - vo...*

den Kopf mehr   in die Hö-he,   da - für die Au-gen
più   al - to   quel col - let - to...   *quel ci - glio un po' più*

senken, die Ar-me in die Mit-te, nun laßt uns sehn die
bas-so... le ma-ni sot-to il pet-to, ve-dre-mo po-scia il

Schrit-te, ge-hen Sie auf und ab, nun laßt uns sehn die Schrit-te,____ ge-hen Sie auf und ab.
pas-so, quando sa-re-te in piè, ve-dre-mo po-scia il pas-so,____ quan-do sa-re-te in piè.

Bli-cke, so schön und doch voll Tü-cke! Wenn den die Frau-en lie - ben, so wis-sen sie war-um,
tu - ra, che vez - zo, che fi - gu - ra! Se l'a-ma-no le fem-mi-ne, han cer-to il lor per - chè,

so wis-sen sie, so wis-sen sie war-um, ja, ja, die Frau-en wis-sen gar wohl war-
se l'a-ma-no, han cer-to il lor per-chè, han cer-to, cer-to, cer-to il lor per-

Recitativo

145

attacca subito il Terzetto [Nº 13]

Sechste Szene

[Susanna (beiseite). Die Vorigen.]
[Susanna tritt ein und bleibt an der Schwelle, da sie
den Grafen an der Tür des Kabinettes erblickt]

Scena VI

[I suddetti, Susanna (in disparte).]
[La Susanna entra per la porta ond'è uscita, e si ferma, vedendo
il Conte, che dalla porta del gabinetto sta favellando]

Nº 13. Terzetto

Recitativo

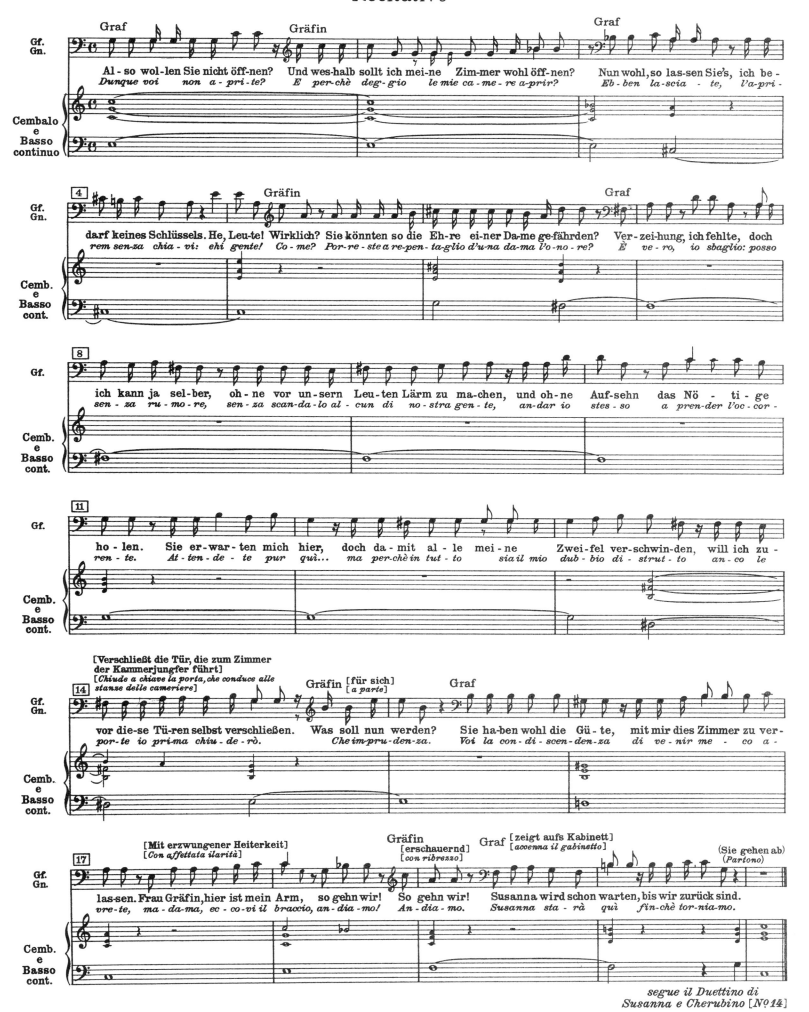

segue il Duettino di
Susanna e Cherubino [Nº 14]

Siebente Szene

[Susanna (kommt schnell aus dem Alkoven).
Dann Cherubino (der aus dem Kabinett kommt)]

Scena VII

[Susanna (uscendo dall' alcova in fretta),
poi Cherubino (ch'esce dal gabinetto).]

№ 14. Duettino

[Susanna stößt einen hohen Schrei aus, setzt sich einen Augenblick und geht dann zum Balkon]
[Susanna mette un alto grido, siede un momento, poi va al balcone]

Recitativo

Achte Szene   Scena VIII

Die Gräfin. Der Graf.   La Contessa, il Conte.

[Der Graf mit Hammer und Stemmeisen in der Hand;
bei seinem Eintritt untersucht er alle Türen]

[Il Conte con martello, e tenaglia in mano;
al suo arrivo esamina tutte le porte]

segue Finale [Nº15]

№ 15. Finale

Neunte Szene

[Susanna. Die Vorigen.]

(Susanna kommt aus der Tür und bleibt ernsthaft stehen)

Scena IX

[I suddetti, e la Susanna.]

(Susanna esce sulla porta tutta grave, ed ivi si ferma)

176

Zehnte Szene
[Figaro. Die Vorigen.]

Scena X
[I suddetti, e Figaro.]

194

Elfte Szene
Scena XI

[Antonio (der Gärtner, mit einem zertretenen Nelkenstock). Die Vorigen.] [I suddetti, Antonio (giardiniere, con un vaso di garofani schiacciato.)]

Zwölfte Szene
[Marcellina. Basilio. Bartolo. Die Vorigen.]

Scena XII
[I suddetti, Marcellina, Bartolo e Basilio]

S.
Schmach, kam der Teu - fel_ aus der Höl - le,_ uns zu brin - gen die - se
tar, cer - to un dia - vol_ dell' in - fer - no_ quì li ha fat - ti ca - pi -

Gn.
Kam der Teu - fel_ aus der Höl - le,_ uns zu brin - gen, zu brin - gen die - se
cer - to un dia - vol_ dell' in - fer - no_ quì li ha fat - ti, li ha fat - ti ca - pi -

M.
Tag, güt' - ge Ster - ne strahl - ten nie - der, brach - ten Glück an die - sem
tar, qual - che nu - me a noi pro - pi - zio quì ci ha fat - ti ca - pi -

Bas.
Tag, güt' - ge Ster - ne_ strahl - ten nie - der,_ brach - ten Glück an die - sem
tar, qual - che nu - me a_ noi pro - pi - zio_ quì ci ha fat - ti ca - pi -

Gf.
Tag, güt' - ge Ster - ne strahl - ten nie - der, brach - ten Glück an die - sem
tar, qual - che nu - me a noi pro - pi - zio quì li ha fat - ti ca - pi -

Brt.
Tag, güt' - ge Ster - ne strahl - ten nie - der, brach - ten Glück an die - sem
tar, qual - che nu - me a noi pro - pi - zio quì ci ha fat - ti ca - pi -

F.
Kam der Teu - fel aus der Höl - le, uns zu brin - gen, zu brin - gen die - se
cer - to un dia - vol dell' in - fer - no quì li ha fat - ti, li ha fat - ti ca - pi -

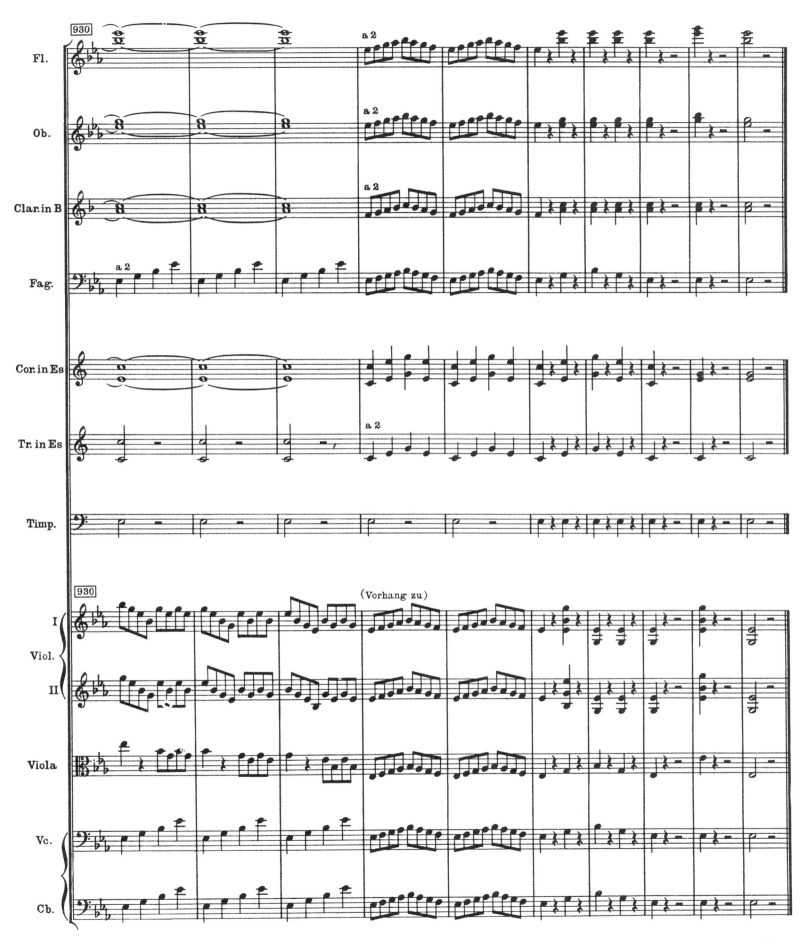

Ende des zweiten Aktes
Fine dell' Atto secondo

DRITTER AKT
[Ein reicher, zur Hochzeitsfeier geschmückter Saal
mit zwei Thronsesseln.]

Erste Szene
Der Graf (allein).

ATTO TERZO
[Sala ricca, con due troni, e preparata
a festa nuziale.]

Scena I
Il Conte (solo).

Recitativo

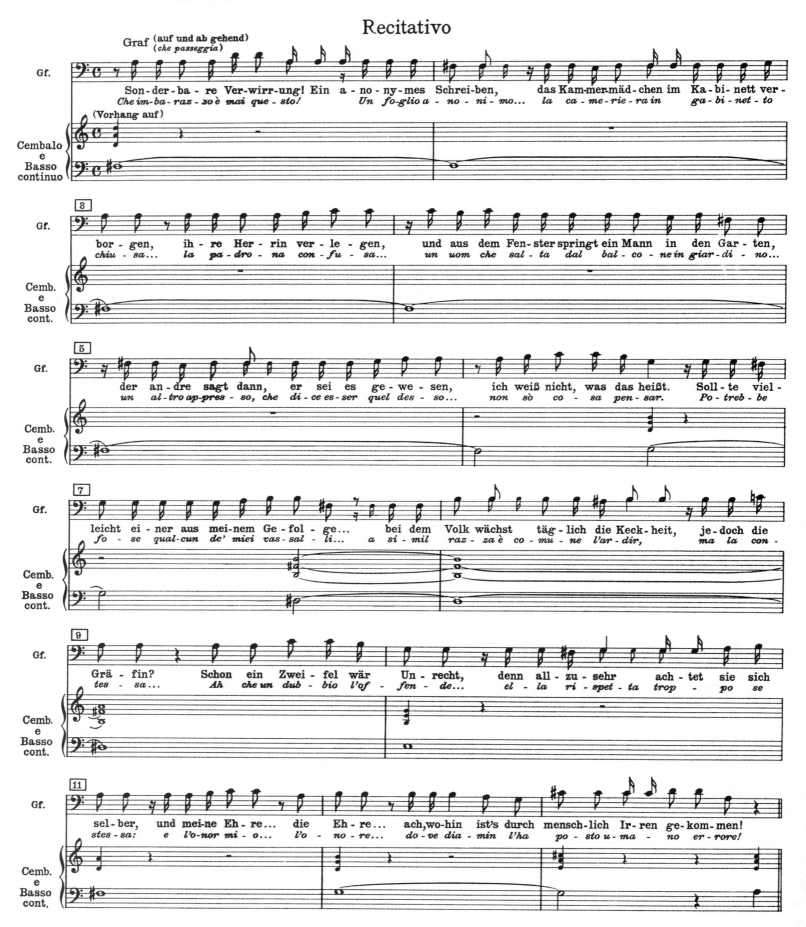

Graf (auf und ab gehend) (che passeggia)

Son-der-ba-re Ver-wirr-ung! Ein a-no-ny-mes Schrei-ben, das Kam-mer-mäd-chen im Ka-bi-nett ver-
Che im-ba-raz-zo è mai que-sto! Un fo-glio a-no-ni-mo... la ca-me-rie-ra in ga-bi-net-to

(Vorhang auf)

bor-gen, ih-re Her-rin ver-le-gen, und aus dem Fen-ster springt ein Mann in den Gar-ten,
chiu-sa... la pa-dro-na con-fu-sa... un uom che sal-ta dal bal-co-ne in giar-di-no...

der an-dre sagt dann, er sei es ge-we-sen, ich weiß nicht, was das heißt. Soll-te viel-
un al-tro ap-pres-so, che di-ce es-ser quel des-so... non sò co-sa pen-sar. Po-treb-be

leicht ei-ner aus mei-nem Ge-fol-ge... bei dem Volk wächst täg-lich die Keck-heit, je-doch die
fo-se qual-cun de' miei vas-sal-li... a si-mil raz-za è co-mu-ne l'ar-dir, ma la con-

Grä-fin? Schon ein Zwei-fel wär Un-recht, denn all-zu-sehr ach-tet sie sich
tes-sa... Ah che un dub-bio l'of-fen-de... el-la ri-spet-ta trop-po se

sel-ber, und mei-ne Eh-re... die Eh-re... ach, wo-hin ist's durch mensch-lich Ir-ren ge-kom-men!
stes-sa: e l'o-nor mi-o... l'o-no-re... do-ve dia-min l'ha po-sto u-ma-no er-ro-re!

Zweite Szene

Der Graf. Die Gräfin und Susanna (im Hintergrund, [vom Grafen unbemerkt]).

Scena II

Il suddetto, la Contessa e la Susanna ([s'arrestano] in fondo [alla scena non vedute dal Conte]).

32 Susanna

mir? Herr Graf, die gnäd'ge Grä-fin, sie lei-det an heft'-gem Kopf-weh, und sie läßt um ihr
co-sa? Si-gnor... la vo-stra spo-sa hai so-li-ti va-po-ri, e vi chie-de il fia-

Cemb. e Basso cont.

35 Graf   Susanna   Graf

Riech-fläsch-chen bit-ten. Hier ist es. Ich bring's gleich wie-der. Nein, nein, du kannst es ja für dich be-
schet-to de-gli o-do-ri. Pren-de-te. Or vel ri-por-to. Eh no, po-te-te ri-te-ner-lo per

Cemb. e Basso cont.

38 Susanna   Graf

hal-ten. Für mich? Das sind kei-ne Lei-den für Mäd-chen mei-nes Stan-des. Ei-ne
voi. Per me? Que-sti non son ma-li da don-ne tri-via-li. Un' a-

Cemb. e Basso cont.

40   Susanna

Braut, die am Ta-ge ih-rer Hoch-zeit den Bräu-ti-gam ver-lie-ren soll? Wenn von der Mit-gift, die Sie mir ver-spro-chen,
man-te, che per-de il ca-ro spo-so sul pun-to d'ot-te-ner-lo. Pa-gan-do Mar-cel-li-na col-la do-te,

Cemb. e Basso cont.

43   Graf   Susanna   Graf

Mar-cel-li-na ich be-zah-le? Die ich ver-spro-chen, wann denn? Ich glaubt Sie so zu ver-ste-hen. Ja, wenn du mich nur
che voi mi pro-met-te-ste. Ch'io vi pro-mi-si, quan-do? Cre-dea d'a-ver-lo in-te-so. Sì, se vo-lu-to a-

Cemb. e Basso cont.

46   Susanna

hät-test recht ver-ste-hen wol-len! Ich kenn mei-ne Pflich-ten, was Ex-zel-lenz be-feh-len, das tu ich ger-ne.
ve-ste in-ten-der me voi stes-sa. È mio do-ve-re: e quel di sua Ec-cel-len-za è il mio vo-le-re.

Cemb. e Basso cont.

attacca subito il Duettino
di Susanna ed il Conte [N⁰ 16]

№ 16. Duettino

Recitativo

Dritte Szene

Figaro. Susanna. Dann gleich wieder der Graf.

Scena III

Figaro, Susanna, e subito il Conte.

segue Recitativo istrumentato del Conte ed Aria [Nº 17]

Vierte Szene
[Der Graf (allein).]

Scena IV
[Il Conte (solo).]

N⁰ 17. Recitativo ed Aria

Recitativo
[Maestoso]

2 Flauti

2 Oboi

2 Fagotti

2 Corni in D

2 Trombe in D

Timpani in D und A

Violino I

Violino II

Viola

Graf
Il Conte

Der Pro-zeß schon ge-won-nen?
Hai già vin-ta la cau-sa!

Ha, was hör ich?
Co-sa sen-to!

Al-so war dies ein Fallstrick?
In qual lac-cio io ca-de-a?

Violoncello

Contrabasso

5 Presto

Ob.

Fag.

Cor. in D

5 Presto

Viol. I

Viol. II

Viola

Gf.

Schänd-li-che,
Per-fi-di,

ich will euch,
io vo-glio...

ich will euch auf das Strengste be-strafen;
io vo-glio di tal mo-do pu-nir-vi,

Vc.

Cb.

Aria

spotten mich ob mei - ner Lie - bes-glut.
ri - de - re di mia in - fe - li - ci - tà.
Darf ich der Hoffnung le - ben,
Già la spe - ran - za so - la
Rache an dir zu
del - le ven - det - te

nehmen, fühl ich die Brust sich he - ben, wallt hei - ßer mir das Blut, wallt heiß das Blut, wallt
mi - e quest' a - ni - ma con - so - la, e giu - bi - lar mi fa, e giu - bi - lar, e

Fünfte Szene
Der Graf. Marcellina. Don Curzio. Figaro.
Bartolo. [Später Susanna.]

Scena V
Il Conte. Marcellina. Don Curzio. Figaro
e Bartolo. [Poi Susanna.]

Recitativo

21

Brt. / F. / Gf. / M. / D.C.

Figaro — Graf — Marcellina — Bartolo — Don Curzio

ar-mes Findelkind? Nein, Herr Doktor, ver-lo-ren und dann geraubt. Wie denn? Wo denn? Be-wei-se! Ja die Be-
bin tro-va-to? No per-du-to, dot-tor, an-zi ru-ba-to. Co-me? Co-sa? La pro-va? Il te-sti-

Cemb. e Basso cont.

24

D.C. / F.

Figaro

wei-se! Gold, ed-le Stei-ne und reich-ge-stick-te Tü-cher, die bei dem hilf-lo-sen Kin-de die Stra-ßen-räu-ber
mo-nio? L'o-ro, le gem-me, e i ri-ca-ma-ti pan-ni, che ne' più te-ne-ri an-ni mi ri-tro-va-ro a-

Cemb. e Basso cont.

27

F.

fan-den und raub-ten, das sind ge-nug Be-wei-se mei-ner a-dli-gen Her-kunft, und dann vor al-lem auf mei-nem
des-so i ma-sna-die-ri, so-no g'in-di-zi ve-ri di mia na-sci-tà il-lu-stre: e so-pra-tut-to questo al mio

Cemb. e Basso cont.

30

F. / M.

Marcellina — Figaro — Marcellina

Ar-me ein hieroglyph'sches Zeichen. Ei-ne Spatel auf dem rechten Arme? Woher wissen Sie das? O Himmel, er
braccio im-presso ge-ro-gli-fi-co... U-na spa-tola impressa al braccio destro... E a voi ch'il dis-se? Oh Di-o, è

Cemb. e Basso cont.

33

M. / F. / D.C. / Gf. / Brt.

Figaro — Don Curzio — Graf — Bartolo — Marcinella — Bartolo — Figaro — Bartolo

ist es! Ja freilich bin ich's. Wer? Wer? Wer? Unser Rafa-el. Und Räuber stahlen dich? Bei ei-nem Schlosse. Hier deine
e-gli... È ver son i-o. Chi? Chi? Chi? Ra-fa-el-lo. E i la-dri ti ra-pir...Pres-so un ca-stel-lo. Ec-co tua

Cemb. e Basso cont.

36

Brt. / F. / D.C. / Gf. / M.

Figaro — Bartolo — Don Curzio und Graf — Figaro — Marcellina

Mut-ter! Mei-ne Am-me? Nein, die Mut-ter! Die Mut-ter? Was hör ich? Hier steht dein Va-ter!
ma-dre. Ba-li-a... No, tua ma-dre. Sua ma-dre! Co-sa sen-to! Ec-co tuo pa-dre.

Cemb. e Basso cont.

attacca subito il Sestetto [Nº 18]

№ 18. Sestetto

Sechste Szene
Susanna. Marcellina. Figaro. Bartolo.

Scena VI
Susanna, Marcellina, Figaro e Bartolo.

Recitativo

Marcellina: Sehn Sie, mein lieber Doktor, in ihm den Spröß-ling un-srer al-ten Lie-be. Re-den wir
Ec- co-vi, o ca-ro a-mi-co, il dol-ce frut-to dell' an-ti- co a-mor no-stro... Or non par-

nicht von so ur-al-ten Ge-schich-ten. Er ist mein Jun-ge, du wirst mei-ne Gat-tin, und die Hoch-zeit mag sein, so-bald ihr
lia-mo di fat-ti sì ri-mo-ti, e-gli è mio fi-glio, mia con-sor-te voi sie-te; e le noz-ze fa-rem quan-do vo-

Marcellina: wollt. Heut noch, heut sei Dop-pel-hoch-zeit. [Gibt Figaro das Billett] [Dà il biglietto a Figaro] Nimm hier, es ist der Schuld-schein, den du mir einst ge-
le-te. Og-gi, e dop-pie sa-ran-no: pren-di, que-sto è il bi-gliet-to del de-nar che a me

Susanna: [wirft eine Börse auf die Erde] [getta per terra una borsa di danari] Bartolo: [desgleichen] [fa lo stesso] Figaro:
ge-ben, er sei die Mit-gift. Nimm auch hier die-se Bör-se. Und hier noch ei-ne. Bra-vo, werft im-mer her, ich kann's ge-
de-vi, ed è tua do-te. Pren-di an-cor que-sta bor-sa. E que-sta an-co-ra. Bra-vi, git-ta-te pur, ch'io pi-glio o-

Susanna: brau-chen. Nun wol-len wir der Grä-fin und An-to-nio die Ge-schich-te gleich er-zäh-len. Wer ist wie ich so
gno-ra. Vo-lia-mo ad in-for-mar d'o-gni av-ven-tu-ra Ma-da-ma, e no-stro zi-o. Chi al par di me con-

Siebente Szene
Barbarina. Cherubino.

Scena VII
Barbarina, Cherubino.

Barbarina

Ge-schwind, komm mit, schö-ner Pa - ge, in un-serm Hau-se fin-dest du schon ver-sam-melt die schön-sten Mäd-chen und
An - diam, an - diam, bel pag-gio, in ca-sa mi - a tut-te ri-tro-ve-ra - i le più bel-le ra-

Frau-en aus dem Schlos-se, von al-len wirst du wohl die schön - ste sein. Ach, wenn der Graf mich dort
gaz - ze del ca - stel - lo, di tut - te sa - rai tu cer-to il più bel - lo. Ah, se il Con - te mi

fän - de, dann we-he mir, du weißt, er glaubt, ich sei längst schon nach Se - vil - la. Was gibt's denn da be-
tro - va, mi - se - ro me, tu sai che par-ti - to ei mi cre - de per Si - vi - glia. Oh ve' che ma-ra-

sondres? Wenn er dich fän - de, so wär's ja nichts neu-es. Hö - re! Wir zie - hen dir Klei-der an von uns hier, und dann
vi - glia, e se ti tro-va non sa - rà co-sa nuo-va... O - di... Vo - glia-mo ve-stir-ti co-me no - i: tut-te in-

gehn wir zu-sam-men, um der Frau Grä-fin Blu-men zu brin-gen. Ver-trau-e, o Che-ru-bin, auf Bar-ba - ri-na!
siem an-drem poi a pre-sen-tar de' fio-ri a Ma - da-mi - na; fi-da-ti, o Che-ru-bin, di Bar-ba - ri-na.

[Sie gehen ab]
[Partono]

[segue Recitativo istromentato
con Aria della Contessa Nº 19]

Achte Szene
[Die Gräfin (allein).]

Scena VIII
[La Contessa (sola).]

№ 19. Recitativo ed Aria

segue l'Aria della Contessa

wie - - - - der-kehrt, mir wie - der-kehrt, mir wie - der - kehrt!
gra - - - to cor, Vin - gra - to_ cor, Vin - gra - to cor!

306

Neunte Szene
Der Graf. Antonio [mit dem Hut Cherubinos in der Hand].

Scena IX
Il Conte, ed Antonio [con cappello in mano].

Recitativo

Zehnte Szene
Die Gräfin. Susanna.

Scena X
La Contessa, e Susanna.

№ 20. Duettino

308

Recitativo

Elfte Szene

[Cherubino (als Landmädchen verkleidet). Barbarina und andere
Landmädchen (alle mit Blumensträußen).] Die Vorigen.

[Cherubino (vestito da contadina), Barbarina, e alcune altre
contadine (vestite del medesimo modo, con mazzetti di fiori) e detti.]

No. 21. Coro

Gnäd'-ge Grä-fin, die-se Ro-sen, so wie Sie, so sanft und schön, pflückten wir am frü-hen
Ri - ce - ve - te, o pa-dron-ci - na, que-ste ro-se, e que-sti fior, che ab-biam col-ti sta-mat-

Ehr-furcht ge - ben kann, die-se Blu-men huldreich an, huld - reich an, neh - men Sie die-se
dia - mo di _ buon cor, ve lo dia-mo di _ buon cor, di buon cor, di buon cor, ve lo

Blu - men huld-reich an.
dia - mo di _ buon cor.

Recitativo

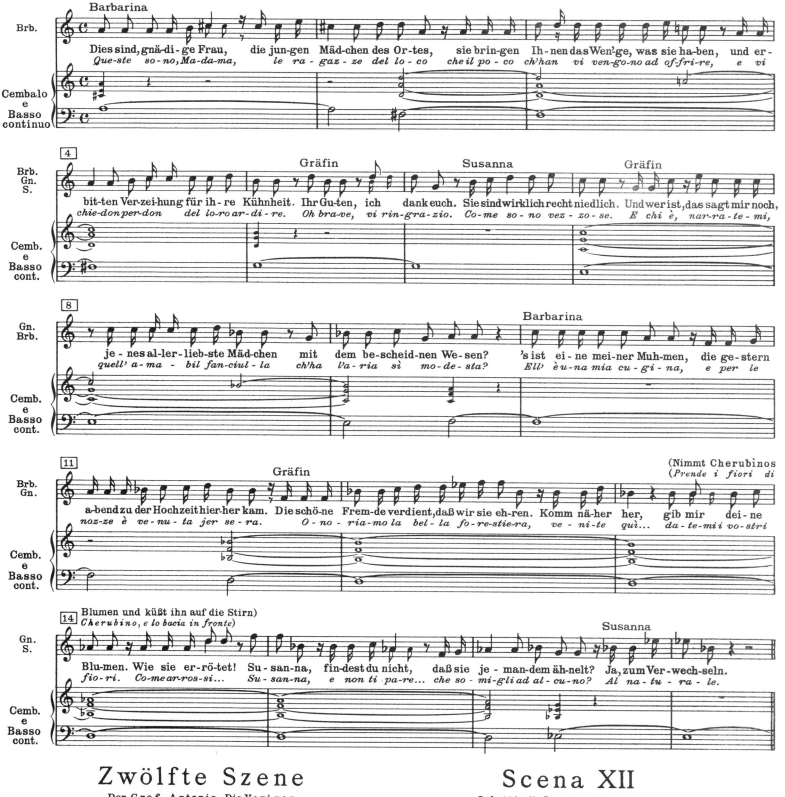

Brb. **Barbarina**
Dies sind, gnä-di-ge Frau, die jun-gen Mäd-chen des Or-tes, sie brin-gen Ih-nen das Wen'-ge, was sie ha-ben, und er-
Que-ste so-no, Ma-da-ma, le ra-gaz-ze del lo-co che il po-co ch'han vi ven-go-no ad of-fri-re, e vi

Brb. Gn. S. **Gräfin** **Susanna** **Gräfin**
bit-ten Ver-zei-hung für ih-re Kühn-heit. Ihr Gu-ten, ich dank euch. Sie sind wirk-lich recht nied-lich. Und wer ist, das sagt mir noch,
chie-don per-don del lo-ro ar-di-re. Oh bra-ve, vi rin-gra-zio. Co-me so-no vez-zo-se. E chi è, nar-ra-te-mi,

Gn. Brb. **Barbarina**
je - nes al-ler-lieb-ste Mäd-chen mit dem be-scheid-nen We-sen? 's ist ei - ne mei-ner Muh-men, die ge-stern
quell' a-ma-bil fan-ciul-la ch'ha l'a-ria sì mo-de-sta? Ell' è u-na mia cu-gi-na, e per le

Brb. Gn. **Gräfin** (Nimmt Cherubinos
(Prende i fiori di
a-bend zu der Hoch-zeit hier-her kam. Die schö-ne Frem-de ver-dient, daß wir sie eh-ren. Komm nä-her her, gib mir dei-ne
noz-ze è ve-nu-ta jer se-ra. O-no-ria-mo la bel-la fo-re-stie-ra, ve-ni-te quì... da-te-mii vo-stri

Gn. S. Blumen und küßt ihn auf die Stirn)
Cherubino, e lo bacia in fronte) **Susanna**
Blu-men. Wie sie er-rö-tet! Su-san-na, fin-dest du nicht, daß sie je - man-dem äh-nelt? Ja, zum Ver-wech-seln.
fio-ri. Co-me ar-ros-si... Su-san-na, e non ti pa-re... che so-mi-glia ad al-cu-no? Al na-tu-ra-le.

Zwölfte Szene

Der Graf. Antonio. Die Vorigen.

[Antonio schleicht sachte herbei, nimmt Cherubino die Haube ab und setzt ihm den Offiziershut auf]

Scena XII

I detti, il Conte, ed Antonio.

[Antonio ha il cappello di Cherubino: entra in scena pian piano, gli cava la cuffia di donna, e gli mette in testa il cappello stesso]

A. Gn. S. Gf. **Antonio** **Gräfin** **Susanna** **Graf** **Gräfin**
Ei, al-le Wet-ter, das ist ja der Herr Haupt-mann. O Him-mel! (Der Ver-weg-ne.) Nun, teu-re Gat-tin! Ich
Eh, co-spet-tac-cio, è que-sti l'uf-fi-cia-le. Oh stel-le! (Ma-lan-dri-no!) Eb-ben, Ma-da-ma! Io

(s'ode la marcia da lontano e seguita
il Recitativo nella marcia)

№ 22. Finale

322

Vierzehnte Szene

[Der Graf. Die Gräfin. Figaro. Susanna. Marcellina.
Bartolo. Antonio. Barbarina. Jäger (mit Büchsen). Gerichts-
diener. Bauern und Bäuerinnen.]

[Zwei Mädchen, die den mit weißen Federn geschmückten Brauthut
tragen; zwei andere mit dem weißen Schleier, noch zwei andere mit
Handschuhen und Blumenstrauß. Andere Mädchen, welche Hut,
Schleier etc. für Susanna tragen. Susanna wird von Bartolo zum
Grafen geführt; sie kniet nieder, um von ihm den Hut etc. in Empfang
zu nehmen. Figaro führt Marcellina zur Gräfin in derselben
Absicht.]

Scena XIV

[I suddetti, la Contessa, Figaro, Susanna, Marcellina,
Bartolo, Antonio, Barbarina, Cacciatori (con fucile in spalla),
Gente del foro. Contadini e Contadine.]

[Due giovinette, che portano il cappello verginale con piume bianche,
due altre un bianco velo, due altre i guanti e il mazzetto di fiori.
Figaro con Marcellina. Due altre giovinette, che portano un simile
cappello per Susanna ecc. Bartolo con Susanna. Due giovinette
incominciano il coro, che termina in ripieno, Bartolo conduce la
Susanna al Conte, e s'inginocchia per ricever da lui il cappello ecc.
Figaro conduce Marcellina alla Contessa, e fa la stessa funzione.]

attacca subito il Coro

liebten, mit Krän - zen ge - schmückt, be - sin - get ihn herz - lich, der euch so be - glückt, ihr

stan - ti se - gua - ci d'o - nor, can - ta - te, lo - da - te sì sag - gio si - gnor, a -

treu - en Ge - lieb - ten, mit Krän - zen ge - schmückt, be - sin - get ihn herz - lich, der euch so be -

man - ti co - stan - ti se - gua - ci d'o - nor, can - ta - te, lo - da - te sì sag - gio si -

glückt, be-sin-get ihn herz-lich,der euch so be-glückt. Er schützt eu-re Eh-re
gnor,   can-ta - te, lo - da - te sì sag - gio   si-gnor. A un drit - to ce - den - do,

und schont eu-re Un-schuld,   er gibt euch die
che ol - trag - gia,che of - fen - de,   ei ca - ste vi

[Susanna, während des Duettes vor dem Grafen auf den Knien, zupft ihn am Kleid und zeigt ihm das Briefchen; dann greift sie, den Zuschauern sichtbar, nach dem Kopf, wobei sie dem Grafen, welcher anscheinlich ihr den Hut zurechtsetzt, das Briefchen gibt. Der Graf verbirgt es schnell. Susanna steht auf und verneigt sich. Figaro empfängt sie vom Grafen und sie tanzen Fandango; Marcellina steht später auf, Bartolo empfängt sie von der Hand der Gräfin.]

[Susanna essendo in ginocchio durante il duo, tira il Conte per l'abito, gli mostra il bigliettino, dopo passa la mano dall' alto degli spettatori alla testa, dove pare che il Conte le aggiusti il cappello, e le dà il biglietto. Il Conte se lo mette furtivamente in seno, Susanna s'alza, e gli fa una riverenza. Figaro viene a riceverla, e si balla il fandango. Marcellina s'alza un' po'più tardi. Bartolo viene a riceverla dalle mani della Contessa.]

Graf (nimmt das Billett hervor und sticht sich mit der Nadel in
(cava il biglietto e nel aprirlo si punge il dito)

Ja,—— so machen's al-le Wei-ber, man ritzt sich, wo man
Eh —— già so - li - ta u-san-za, le don-ne fic-can

334

attacca subito il Coro

338

Ende des dritten Aktes
Fine dell' Atto terzo

VIERTER AKT
Kabinett

Erste Szene
Barbarina (allein [mit einer Laterne]).

ATTO QUARTO
Gabinetto

Scena I
Barbarina (sola [tenendo una lanterna di carta]).

№ 23. Cavatina

attacca Recitativo

Zweite Szene
Barbarina. Figaro. Marcellina.

Scena II
Barbarina, Figaro, e Marcellina.

Recitativo

Figaro Bar-ba-ri-na, was suchst du? **Barbarina** Ach, ich ha-be sie ver-lo-ren! **Figaro** Was denn? **Marcellina** Was denn? **Barbarina** Die Na-del, die der
Bar-ba-ri-na cos' ha-i? L'ho per-du-ta, cu-gi-no. Co-sa? Co-sa? La spil-la, che a me

Graf mir ge-ge-ben, sie Su-san-na zu brin-gen. **Figaro** Für Su-san-na, die Na-del? **[Zornig] [In collera]** Ach sieh an, lie-be
die-de il pa-dro-ne per re-car a Su-san-na. A Su-san-na... la spil-la? E co-sì te-ne-

Klei-ne, du ver-stehst schon die Kunst, **(Faßt sich) (Si calma)** al-les treff-lich zu ma-chen, was du an-fängst. **Barbarina** Was ist, war-um so
rel-la il me-stie-ro già sa-i... di far tut-to sì ben quel che tu fa-i? Cos' è, vai me-co in

[Sucht einen Augenblick auf dem Fußboden, nachdem er vorher aus der Haube oder dem Kleid Marcellinas geschickt eine Nadel herausgezogen hatte, und reicht sie nun Barbarina]
[Cerca un momento per terra, dopo aver destramente cavata una spilla dall' abito, o dalla cuffia di Marcellina, e la da a Barbarina]

bö-se? **Figaro** Siehst du nicht, daß ich scher-ze? Ei sieh nur, da ist die Na-del, die der gnäd'ge Herr dir gab, um Su-san-na sie zu
col-le-ra? E non ve-di ch'io scher-zo? Os-ser-va... que-sta è la spil-la che il Con-te da re-ca-re ti die-de al-la Su-

brin-gen, sie dien-te als Sie-gel ei-nem Brief-chen. Siehst du nun, ich weiß al-les. **Barbarina** War-um fragst du denn
san-na, e ser-via di si-gil-lo a un bi-gliet-ti-no; ve-di s'io so-no in-strut-to. E per-chè il chie-di a

mich, wenn du al-les weißt? **Figaro** Ei, ich woll-te nur hö-ren, wie der Graf den Auf-trag dir ge-ge-ben. **Barbarina** Je nun, er sag-te mir:
me quan-do sai tut-to? A-vea gu-sto d'u-dir co-me il pa-dro-ne ti diè la com-mis-sio-ne. Che mi-ra-co-li!

Dritte Szene
Marcellina. Figaro.

Scena III
Marcellina, e Figaro.

Vierte Szene
Marcellina (allein).

Scena IV
Marcellina (sola).

segue l'Aria di Marcellina [Nº 24]

Nº 24. Aria

Die Zie - ge und der
Il ca-pro,e la ca-

Ziegenbock sind fried-lich je-der - zeit,__ das Schäfchen und auch sein Lämmchen, sie ken - nen kei-nen Streit.__ Ja
pret - ta son sem-pre in a-mi - stà,__ l'a-gnel-lo all'a-gnel-let - ta la guer-ra mai non fà.__ Le

Sechste Szene

Figaro [allein]. Dann Basilio, Bartolo und ein Trupp Arbeiter.

[Figaro im Mantel mit einer Nachtlaterne]

Scena VI

Figaro [solo], poi Basilio, Bartolo, e truppa di lavoratori.

[Figaro con mantello, e lanternino notturno]

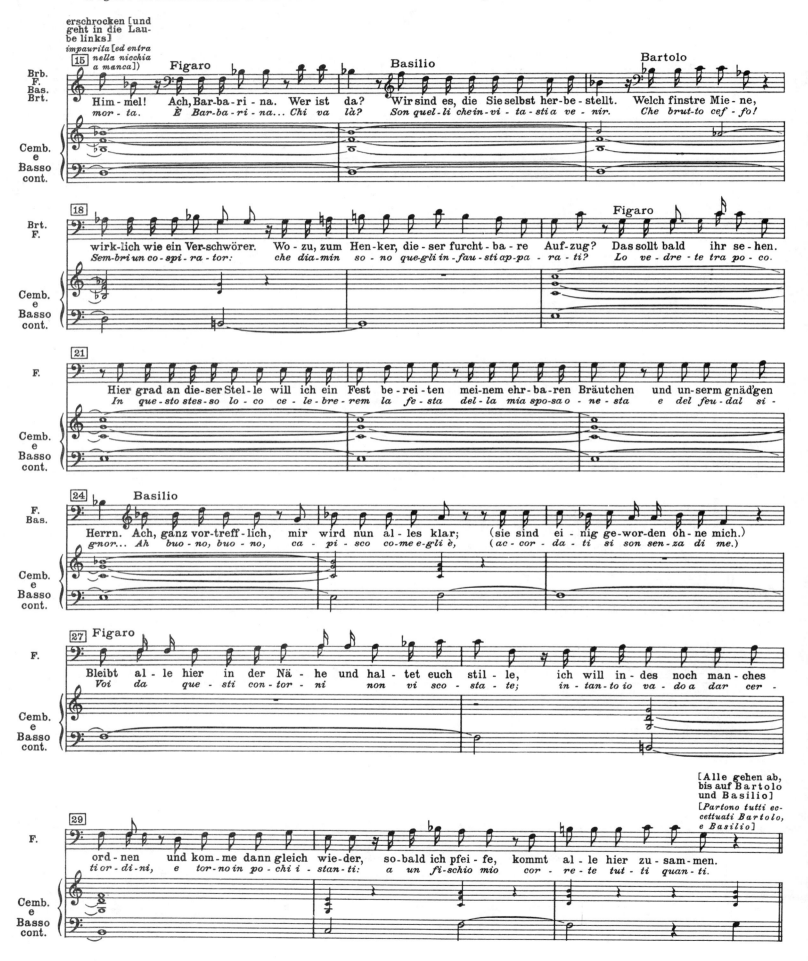

Siebente Szene
Basilio. Bartolo.

Scena VII
Basilio e Bartolo.

segue l'Aria di Basilio [Nº 25]

Nº 25. Aria

Achte Szene
[Figaro (allein)]

Scena VIII
[Figaro (solo)]

№ 26. Recitativo ed Aria

Al-les ist rich-tig, auch kann die Stun-de nicht mehr fern sein; ich hö-re kom-men... Sie ist es! Nein, 's war
Tut-to è dis-po-sto: l'o-ra do-vreb-be es-ser vi-ci-na; io sen-to gen-te. È des-sa... non è al-

nichts; die Nacht ist dun-kel. Ich trei-be al-so heu-te das al-ler-lieb-ste Handwerk des ei-fer-sücht'-gen
cun... bu-ja è la not-te... ed io co-mincio o-ma-i, a fa-re il sci-mu-ni-to me-stie-ro di ma-

Neunte Szene

Die Gräfin und Susanna [beide verkleidet]. Marcellina.

Scene IX

Susanna, la Contessa [travestite], Marcellina.

Recitativo

Zehnte Szene

Figaro (beiseite). Die Vorigen.

Scene X

I suddetti, Figaro (in disparte).

segue Recitativo istromentato
con Rondò di Susanna [Nº 27]

№ 27. Recitativo ed Aria

Recitativo

End-lich naht sich die Stunde, da ich
Giunse al-fin il mo-men-to che go-

dich, o Ge-lieb-ter, bald ganz be-si-tzen werde!
drò senz'af-fan-no in brac-cio all' i-dol mi-o.

Ängst-li-che Sor-gen, ent-flieht aus mei-nem Her-zen, stört nicht län-ger die heiß-er-sehn-ten
Ti - mi-de cu-re, u - sci-te dal mio pet-to, a tur-bar nonve-ni-te il mio di-

Elfte Szene
Die Vorigen. Dann Cherubino.

Scena XI
I suddetti, e poi Cherubino.

Recitativo

Figaro

F. Schänd-li-che, in sol-cher Wei-se mich zu be-trü-gen! Wach ich o - der
Per - fi - da, ein quel-la for - ma me co men - ti - a? Non so s'io ve - glio, o

Cembalo e Basso continuo

Cher. (kommt singend)
(cantando)

F. Ch. Gn. träum ich? La la la la la
dor - mo. La la la la la lera

Der klei - ne Pa - ge.
Il pic - ciol pag - gio.

Ich hö - re kom-men, jetzt schnell hin - ein zu Bar - ba -
Io sen - to gen - te, en - tria - mo o - ve en - trò Bar - ba -

Gräfin

Cherubino

Cemb. e Basso cont.

Ch. Gn. ri - na. Da seh ich ei - ne
ri - na. Oh ve - do qui u - na

Da - me. O weh mir Ar - men!
don - na. Ahi - mè me - schi - na!

Ist's Täuschung, nach ih - rem Hüt-chen, wenn das
M'in - gan - no, a quel cap - pel - lo, che nell'

Gräfin

Cherubino

Cemb. e Basso cont.

Gräfin

Ch. Gn. Dun - kel nicht täuscht, ist es Su - san - na. Wenn der Graf jetzt er - schien, ich wär ver - lo - ren.
om - bra veggo io par mi Su - san - na. E se il Con - te o - ra vien, sor - te ti - ran - na!

Cemb. e Basso cont.

№ 28. Finale

Zwölfte Szene
[Der Graf. Die Vorigen.]

Scena XII
[I suddetti, il Conte.]

Dreizehnte Szene

Scena XIII

[Susanna. Figaro]

[Figaro, e Susanna]

126
Fl.
Clar. in B
Fag.
Cor. in Es
Viol. I
Viol. II
Viola
F.
Vc.
Cb.
kom - men wie ge - ru - fen, kaum kann ich mich er - ho - len, Su - san-na ist mit dem
tem - po quì giun - ge - te... ve - dre - te là voi stes - sa... il Con - te, e la mia
131
Gra-fen, je-doch Sie sol-len al - les mit eig - nen Au-gen sehn, mit eig-nen Au - gen
spo-sa... di pro - pria man la co - sa toc-car io vi fa-rò, toc - car io vi fa -

Vierzehnte Szene
[Der Graf. Die Vorigen.]

Scena XIV
[I suddetti, poi il Conte.]

Letzte Szene

[Die Vorigen. Bartolo. Antonio. Basilio. Don Curzio.
Diener (mit Fackeln). Dann Susanna, Marcellina, Cherubino,
Barbarina. Später die Gräfin.]

Scena ultima

[I suddetti, Bartolo, Antonio, Basilio, Don Curzio,
Servitori (con fiaccole accese); poi Susanna, Marcellina,
Cherubino, Barbarina; indi la Contessa.]

425

432

435

Ende der Oper
Fine dell' Opera

BASIS OF THE EDITION

The present score is based on Mozart's own manuscript, in the collection of the Prussian State Library in Berlin. Unfortunately this manuscript is not preserved in its entirety; it lacks the recitative "Dunque voi non aprite?" following the Trio No. 13, and the recitative "Tutto è disposto" preceding Figaro's Aria No. 26, both replaced in the manuscript by a copyist's work. Also missing are the recitative "Perfida, e in quella forma meco mentia" preceding the Finale No. 28, and the wind and brass parts of the same Finale from measure 335 to the end, which were written on an "extra sheet." For editing these missing passages, especially the wind and brass parts, it was possible to consult a few old copies—principally the one in the Prince Fürstenberg Library in Donaueschingen—which helped clear up many doubts. The autograph manuscript is very clearly written, but contains many slips of the pen and minor errors of the type commonly made while writing down music. Most of these errors leave no doubt about the correct readings and have been tacitly corrected. Where this was not possible and no comparison with similar passages could be made, the obviously correct versions have been incorporated into the text, whereas all other deviations from the autograph, the correctness of which was not sufficiently established, have been listed without exception in the following Editors' Commentary in order to present as faithful a picture as possible of Mozart's manuscript.

The libretto of the first performance, of which only one copy exists in Washington and one in Florence, could not be consulted because of the war. For the Italian text and stage directions, the edition of the libretto printed in Florence in 1788 was used. Mozart wrote Italian very accurately; here for the first time his punctuation, which makes rich and varied use of semicolons, colons and dashes, has been faithfully followed. Only in the arias and ensembles does Mozart become less careful, and for these the punctuation has been altered or supplied on the basis of the libretto. When, as it sometimes happens, the text in the autograph differs from that in the printed libretto, the version of the autograph has been considered as authoritative, and changes have been made correspondingly.

Mozart transferred Da Ponte's stage directions to the autograph only partially; on the other hand, in many places he added stage directions himself or changed some. All missing stage directions necessary for actual production have been supplied from the libretto, but placed in square brackets to show their origin clearly.

Slurs, ties and staccato marks missing in the autograph have been supplied tacitly when analogous passages or the notation of the other instruments proved them to be necessary.

Mozart's autograph contains dots, short heavy dashes and long thin dashes. In Mozart, however, the short heavy dash is not a staccato mark in our modern sense, but an accent, a "ben marcato." At any rate, in the autograph the difference between dots and dashes is not firm; many long dashes occur in places where there is no doubt, or else it is highly probable, that they signify accents, whereas certain dots are abbreviated dashes (in general Mozart scarcely seems to make a basic distinction between dots and weak dashes). However, in order to rule out any doubts, the autograph has been scrupulously followed here, insofar as possible, since the pen is more sensitive than the engraving tool.

EDITORS' COMMENTARY

Sinfonia

Meas. 73/74: In the autograph manuscript [referred to simply as "MS" in this Commentary], the First Violins have no slur.

M. 76: In the MS, the natural sign in front of the c^2 in the Second Violins is missing.

M. 90: In the MS, Clarinet II has no tie.

Mm. 96/97: In the MS, the slur in the First and Second Violins is divided between the measures; later it appears as here.

Mm. 105/106: The slur in the bass is supplied on the basis of mm. 218/219.

M. 106: The staccato mark on the 3rd and 4th quarter notes in the Bassoon have been supplied by the editors.

M. 120: In the MS, the Flute has e^3 instead of a^2.

Mm. 121/122: The staccato mark has been added on the 4th quarter in Flute and Bassoon.

Mm. 123ff.: In the MS, the f and p in the Second Violins and Violas are first written separately as here, later together.

Mm. 139–155: Not written out in the MS, but called for by "da capo 17 Takte."

M. 172: The staccato mark in the Violas is supplied on the basis of m. 59.

M. 181: In the MS, the First Violins have a full rest (see m. 60).

M. 187: In the MS, the Oboes have no slur or tie to the next measure.

M. 203: In the MS, Oboe II has no tie to the next measure.

Mm. 218/219: The staccato marks in the Bassoon part are supplied (see mm. 105/106).

M. 220: The staccato dots for the Second Violins are supplied on the basis of m. 107.

M. 244: In the MS, the Oboes have no tie to the next measure.

Mm. 253–255: A few staccato marks are supplied.

Mm. 266–279: Not written out in the MS, but called for by a ‖: :‖

M. 281: In contrast to mm. 263 and 277, the MS here notates the terminating notes of the trill as 32nd notes.

No. 1. Duettino

Mm. 5–7: The dynamic mark has been supplied for the Violas; missing in the MS.

M. 7: In the MS, Oboe II lacks the slur.

M. 8: The indications for Flute and Oboe, missing in the MS, are supplied.

M. 35: Here, and in mm. 54 and 74, the staccato dots for the First and Second Violins are supplied; partially also in the winds, mm. 76 and 79/80.

M. 52: In the MS, the Violas have no tie to the next measure.

Mm. 58/59: In the MS, the Bassoons and bass have no slurs.

Mm. 67ff.: The Bassoon slurs, partially lacking in the MS, are supplied from the Clarinet part.

No. 2. Duettino

Mm. 3ff.: The markings in the Bassoon part, often missing in the MS, are supplied from the First Violin part.

M. 45: Here, and in mm. 49/50, the MS shows no staccato marks for the First Violins.

Mm. 74–77: The legato marks for Bassoon II are supplied.

Mm. 93/94: The MS lacks the slur in Bassoon I (as well as m. 95 in the Bassoon).

Mm. 94/95: The staccato mark in the First Violin part is supplied.

Mm. 116–119: In the MS, the bass has only sf (but see mm. 108–111).

M. 127: In the MS, the staccato mark is missing in the First and Second Violins (in m. 132 it is indicated only in the First Violin part).

M. 134: In the MS, the staccato mark in the Viola part is missing.

No. 3. Cavatina

M. 42: The Horns have sf in the MS.

M. 45: In the MS, the Horns here have another tie to the next measure.

M. 54: The staccato dots in the strings are supplied.

Mm. 65–70: A few of the staccato dots in the First Violins are supplied.

Mm. 72–74: In the MS, the Bassoons have no slur.

M. 98: The MS lacks the Viola legato slur to the next measure.

M. 124: The MS lacks the "arco."

No. 4. Aria (often omitted in performance)

M. 1: The MS has sf in Oboes, Horns, Trumpets and Violas.

Mm. 16/17: The MS lacks the staccato marks in the Horns.

M. 44: In the MS, in the 3rd quarter Oboe I has b^1 and Oboe II has $g\#^1$ (presumably a slip of the pen). The MS places the f in Violin II, Viola and bass on the 3rd quarter.

Mm. 46–49: The MS lacks the slurs for Bassoons and bass.

Mm. 58/59: The MS shows the Oboe II slur only in m. 58.

M. 63: In the MS, Oboe II lacks the tie to the next measure.

M. 74: The MS lacks the slurs in the Horn and Trumpet parts.

M. 79: The bass lacks staccato marks in the MS (as do the Oboes in m. 85, and Bassoons, Second Violins, Violas and bass in m. 86).

Mm. 93–98: In the MS, the Second Violins and Violas have the slurs divided partly by whole measures, partly by half measures.

No. 5. Duettino

M. 12: In the MS, the bass lacks the slur to the next measure.

Mm. 24/25: In the MS, Horn I has no tie (in mm. 26/27 it is missing in both Horns).

Mm. 29–32: In the MS, Horn I lacks the slurs (but see mm. 48–52).

Mm. 36/37: In the MS, the Horns lack the ties (but see mm. 64/65).

M. 63: In the MS, the Bassoons lack the slur (but see m. 59).

M. 67: In the MS, Flute II has no tie to the next measure (but see m. 37).

No. 6. Aria

M. 9: Here and in m. 12 the slurs in the Violas and bass are supplied on the basis of mm. 45 and 48.

Mm. 67/68: In the MS, the Bassoons have only one slur over both measures (in mm. 86/87 the Bassoons have the slur divided by measures, but the Clarinets have only one slur over both measures).

M. 84: In the MS, the fermata is drawn over the note *and* the slur; here it has been divided into two fermatas.

Recitativo:

M. 17: The MS mistakenly has two 16th notes instead of two 8th notes on the 3rd quarter.

No. 7. Terzetto

M. 19: The MS lacks the staccato marks for the First and Second Violins (the same holds for m. 21; in mm. 88 and 90 they are missing in all the strings).

Mm. 29/30: In the MS, the Second Violins have a slur over both measures.

M. 37: The MS lacks the slurs in Bassoon I and Horns.

Mm. 65/66: The MS lacks the ties in the winds.

Mm. 108/109: The MS lacks the slur in the Clarinet part.

Mm. 117–121: The slur in the Bassoon part is supplied.

Mm. 140/141: The legato mark in the Bassoon part is supplied.

Mm. 165/166: In the MS, the Violas have the slur divided by measures (also in mm. 186/187).
Mm. 174/175: The MS lacks the slurs in Clarinet II and Bassoon II.
M. 138: The MS lacks the Horn ties to the next measure (but see m. 165).
M. 190: The MS lacks the staccato marks in the Viola part.
Mm. 201–203: In the MS, the bass slur covers all three measures (also in mm. 204–206).
Mm. 205/206: The MS lacks the Bassoon slurs.

No. 8. Coro

Mm. 1/2: The MS lacks the slurs in the Flutes and First and Second Violins (also in mm. 9/10, 28/29 and 31/32).
M. 11: In the MS, the First Violin slur is divided by half measures.
M. 12: In the MS, the Bassoons have *f* instead of *cresc.*
M. 16: The MS lacks the staccato dots for the Bassoons and bass.
M. 21: The slurs in Bassoons and bass are supplied.
Mm. 22/23: In the MS, the Viola legato mark covers both measures.
M. 24: The MS lacks the Second Violin slur.
M. 28: In the MS, the vocal parts have another *f*.
Mm. 34/36: The staccato dots in the Second Violins and Violas are supplied.
M. 40: Mozart has indicated: "If this chorus is sung a second time, the instrumentation remains the same as the first time."

No. 8a. Coro

M. 1ff.: Only the vocal parts and the bass are notated by Mozart: "gl' Istromenti come prima."

No. 9. Aria

M. 4: In the MS, the 1st quarter for the First Violins consists of a quarter note instead of the 8th note and 8th rest.
Mm. 20–23: In the MS, the Bassoons have a slur over all four measures.
M. 24: The MS lacks the Oboe slur.
Mm. 30/31: The Bassoon slur and Horn tie are supplied.
M. 71: The MS gives the Violas *ff*.

No. 10. Cavatina

M. 1: "Larghetto" is added in another hand.
Mm. 43/44: The Clarinet II tie is supplied on the basis of the Bassoon part.

Recitativo

Here Mozart repeats "Scena I"; later on, as well, the scene division in the present volume differs from that of the MS and the libretto, since stage practice had to be followed.

No. 11. Arietta

M. 1: "Andante" is added in another hand.
Mm. 32/33: The MS lacks the Flute tie (see Clarinet).

No. 12 Aria

M. 12: Here the MS gives the Bassoon slurs in whole measures, later in half measures as printed here.
Mm. 16/17: Here the MS spreads the Flute slur over both measures; later it is divided as in mm. 20/21.
M. 22: The Bassoon II slur is supplied.
M. 31: In the MS, the Oboe I slur starts with m. 32 and ends with m. 33, while m. 34 has a separate slur. The legato marks in Oboe II and Bassoon II in mm. 31–34 are altogether lacking.
M. 40: The MS lacks the Oboe II slur here, in m. 42 and in mm. 44/45 (in m. 45 in Oboe I as well).
M. 41: The staccato dots in the Viola and bass parts are supplied.
M. 45: The MS lacks the Horn I tie to the next measure.
Mm. 50/51: The legato slur for Oboe II is supplied on the basis of Flute I (likewise in the Horns).
Mm. 59/60: The MS lacks the Horn I tie.
Mm. 82–93: The MS lacks the legato marks in Oboe II.

M. 105: The MS lacks the Viola slur (see m. 109).
M. 106: In the MS, the First Violins have the *sfz* on the first note and a slur over the first three notes.
M. 116: The MS here has the Flute and Oboe slur over the 2nd quarter only, in contrast to m. 114.

No. 13. Terzetto

M. 1: The MS lacks the Oboe slur in the 3rd quarter (also in Oboe I, m. 71).
Mm. 10&12: The inconsistency in the First Violin slurs is based on the MS.
M. 34: The MS places the Bassoon and Cello *f* on the 1st quarter (see m. 98).
M. 37: The MS lacks the staccato marks in the bass.
Mm. 46–49: The MS here lacks the slurs in the First and Second Violins, but gives them in mm. 110ff.
Mm. 69/70: The MS lacks the Horn ties.
Mm. 90/91: The Viola slur is supplied.
Mm. 98/99: The MS divides the Bassoon I slur by measures.
M. 114: The MS lacks the bass slur (also in m. 129).

The vocal part of the trio has been printed here as it is sung on the stage. Mozart was fond of noting the highest voice in small ensembles on the topmost staff; according to the grouping at the beginning of the trio, this is the Countess' part. Sometimes the MS indicates a change of singers, but often the Countess is given the higher soprano range with the coloratura, while Susanna's role becomes more secondary. The version of the vocal part as given in the MS, insofar as it differs from the present score, is as follows:

Recitativo

The recitative in the MS is written in another hand than Mozart's. In mm. 6, 11 and 14 of the vocal line, a few obvious slips of the pen have been tacitly corrected.

No. 14. Duettino

M.	7:	The First Violin staccato dots are supplied (also in the Second Violins and Violas on the 3rd and 4th quarters).
Mm.	11ff.:	Mozart is very imprecise from this point on in writing the slurs in the Second Violins and Violas; often the slur is extended to the quarter note of the next measure, often it ends with the measure as here.
M.	13:	Here, and in mm. 28, 39 and 52, a few staccato dots have been supplied.
M.	14:	In the MS, the stage direction is written over both vocal parts.

Recitativo

Mm.   1/2:   The MS has:

but this is crossed out in red. Another hand has changed the first words to "Oh guarda il demonietto," and the following words through "ventre" are deleted, while the Continuo has been corrected to *g*.

No. 15. Finale

M.	5:	The MS places the *p* in the bass on the 2nd quarter.
M.	13:	A few staccato marks here and in m. 15 have been supplied.
M.	52:	The MS gives staccato marks for Flute II [*sic*] and Bassoons only.
M.	57:	The MS lacks the Horn slur (also in m. 60).
Mm.	58/59:	The MS lacks the Horn staccato marks (but see mm.

		55/56).
Mm.	96–99:	A few Viola and bass staccato marks are supplied.
Mm.	113/114:	The MS shows only the tie for Clarinet II (in mm. 115/116 both Clarinets lacks all slurs and ties).
M.	126:	Over the First Violins, the MS gives "Andante di molto"; otherwise it gives "Molto Andante."
M.	135:	Here and in m. 137 the Viola staccato marks are supplied (also for the winds in m. 143).
M.	152:	The MS lacks the Viola tie to the next measure.
M.	154:	The MS lacks the Oboe I slur to the next measure and the Bassoon slur.
M.	161:	The MS lacks the bass staccato marks (also in m. 165).
Mm.	164/165:	The MS lacks the Bassoon legato marks.
Mm.	168–170:	The MS lacks the First Violin staccato dots (those of the Flute, too, in mm. 169/170, those of all the instruments in mm. 181–186, of the First Violins in mm. 271–274—some of the Oboe's and Bassoon's as well—and those of the First Violins and Bassoon in mm. 279–282).
Mm.	176/177:	The MS lacks the Clarinet II and Bassoon slurs (also those for Clarinet II in mm. 178/179).
M.	179:	The MS places staccato marks on the bass on the 2nd–4th quarters.
M.	193:	The Flute slur is supplied (also in m. 269).
Mm.	207/208:	The MS lacks the Flute staccato dots (also in mm. 222/223).
Mm.	209/210:	The MS here lacks the Flute slur, and in mm. 224/225 it is given only on the 3rd and 4th quarters of m. 225 (but see the Oboe part in mm. 295/296).
Mm.	228/229:	The MS lacks the Clarinet slurs.
M.	240:	The slurs in Clarinet I and Bassoon II are supplied.
Mm.	246ff.:	The MS reverses the staves of Susanna and the Countess, so that the Countess would sing the higher part and Susanna the lower.
M.	248:	The MS lacks the Bassoon I slur (also in m. 250).
M.	252:	The MS lacks the Oboe slur.
Mm.	264–266:	The MS lacks the staccato dots in the winds (in the bass, too, in mm. 265/266).
M.	292:	In the MS, the bass has *f* instead of *p cresc.*
M.	293:	In the MS, the *f* in the strings is partly on the 3rd or 4th quarter of m. 292.
M.	304:	The Flute and Oboe [*sic*] slurs are supplied.
M.	312:	In the MS, the Flute has *f* instead of *p cresc.*
Mm.	316/317:	The MS lacks the Flute II tie and slur and the Bassoon II slur.
Mm.	317/318:	The MS gives Clarinet II a tie, surely only by mistake.
M.	321:	The Flute I slur is supplied.
M.	322:	The MS places the *p* for the Countess and Count on the 4th quarter of the preceding measure.
M.	324:	The Flute II and Oboe I slurs are supplied on the basis of the Clarinet part.
Mm.	363–366:	The MS lacks the Oboe II ties.
Mm.	371–374:	The staccato dots in the strings are supplied.
Mm.	375/376:	The MS lacks the Second Violin and Viola slurs (also in mm. 379/380).
Mm.	377/378:	The MS lacks the Second Violin slur (also in mm. 381/382).
M.	389:	In the MS, the *f* for First and Second Violins and Violas is on the 1st 8th note, and in the bass on the 2nd 8th note, as printed here (but see m. 383).
Mm.	399–401:	The MS lacks the Second Violin staccato dots beginning with the 2nd quarter (also in mm. 403-405, from the 2nd quarter of m. 412 through m. 413, and m. 417).
M.	422:	In the MS, the bass has 32nd notes instead of 64th (the Bassoons are instructed to play "col Basso").
Mm.	429/430:	In the MS, the Bassoons have a slur over both measures.
M.	440:	The Flute staccato dots are supplied.
Mm.	441–444:	In the MS, the Horns have no markings.
M.	450:	The MS lacks the Cello slur (also in m. 452).
M.	454:	The MS lacks the Flute and Oboe slurs (also in m. 462).
M.	467:	The MS states: "Fagotti sind extra geschrieben" [The Bassoons are on a separate sheet]. So is the Clarinet part from m. 615 on, although this is not specially pointed out in the MS.
M.	488:	The MS lacks the Second Violin and Viola slur to the next measure.

Mm. 549/550: The Flute slur is supplied.

M. 566: In the MS, the First Violins have a slur over the whole measure.

M. 569: In the MS, the staccato marks are shown only on the First and Second Violins.

Mm. 583/584: The MS lacks the Flute II tie.

M. 594: In the MS, Bassoon II has *a* (parallel octaves).

Mm. 615–617: The MS lacks the Flute slur (also in mm. 623–625).

M. 634: The Bassoon tie to the next measure is supplied (also in m. 636).

M. 638: The MS lacks the Horn I tie to the next measure.

M. 639: In the MS, the Clarinets and Bassoons have *f* instead of *p cresc.* and *cresc.*, respectively, and the Oboe slur is missing.

M. 649: In the MS, the Bassoon has a slur to the next measure.

M. 666: The MS lacks the Clarinet ties to the next measure.

M. 687: In the MS, the bass has a dotted quarter note on the 1st half, which is changed here on the basis of m. 691.

M. 688: In the MS, the Clarinet and Bassoon slurs begin with the next measure, in contrast to m. 692.

M. 696: In the MS, the Oboes and Horns have a quarter note, the Clarinets and Bassoons an 8th note.

M. 697: The MS says: "Scena XII ed ultima." (Also, it is stated in Mozart's hand: "Alle Blas. Instrumenten sind auf dem Extra Blatt" [All wind instruments are on the additional sheet]); they are located in the supplement to the MS.

Mm. 697/698: In the MS, the Trumpets have: [musical notation]. Everywhere else this is changed to the form printed here.

Mm. 711/712: The MS lacks the Clarinet I and Bassoon I slurs.

Mm. 733/734: The MS lacks the Clarinet II tie.

M. 737: In the MS, the Bassoon I slur begins with the next measure.

M. 760: In the MS, the Clarinet I and Bassoon I legato marks extend only to the 2nd half note in the preceding measure.

M. 782: The bass staccato marks are supplied.

M. 786: In the MS, the Flute legato marks begin in the next measure, in contrast to m. 792 (an error due to the turning of a page in the MS). Also, from this measure to the end of the act, the MS reverses the staves of the Count and Bartolo, so that the former would sing the lower part and vice versa.

Mm. 786–788: The MS lacks the legato marks for both Clarinets.

M. 792: In the MS, the Clarinet I legato mark begins with the next measure. That of Clarinet II is totally missing (as is the Bassoon I legato mark in mm. 793/794).

M. 821: The MS has the incorrect Trumpet notes *b♭¹* and *g¹*.

M. 829: The Horn slurs are supplied.

Mm. 854/855: The MS lacks the Clarinet legato mark.

M. 855: In the MS, the First Violin slur is divided by half measures.

Mm. 897/898: The MS lacks the Horn II tie (also in mm. 905/906).

Mm. 915/916: The bass legato mark is supplied on the basis of mm. 907/908.

Recitativo

M. 48: At the end Mozart has noted "attacca il Duetto," although the next number is headed "Duettino."

No. 16. Duettino

Mm. 8/9: The MS lacks the First Violin staccato dots.

M. 21: The MS lacks the Horn ties to the next measure.

M. 25: The Bassoon II slur is supplied.

M. 28: In the MS, the bass has a quarter note and rest instead of the half note.

M. 30: The bass slur is supplied on the basis of m. 55.

M. 36: The MS lacks the Bassoon and First Violin staccato dot here and in mm. 38 and 40.

Mm. 38/39: In contrast to the preceding and following measures, the MS here divides the bass slur by single measures.

M. 51: The MS lacks the First and Second Violin staccato mark (in m. 45 it is given only in the First Violins).

M. 63: In the MS, the Flute slur is divided; it has been altered here by analogy with the Bassoon part.

M. 71: The MS lacks the Flute slur.

No. 17. Recitativo ed Aria

M. 1: "Maestoso" is added in another hand.

M. 33: The Bassoon I slur is supplied.

M. 37: In the MS, the Bassoons have a slur over the whole measure.

Mm. 42/43: In the MS, here and in mm. 49/50, the Oboe has no legato mark (the same holds for the Bassoon in mm. 43/44 and 50/51).

Mm. 44–46: The Flute II and Bassoon II legato mark is supplied on the basis of mm. 51–53, where it is indicated for the Flute.

M. 45: The MS lacks the Bassoon I slur (also in m. 52).

M. 49: In the MS, the Bassoons have a quarter note instead of the 8th note.

Mm. 54/55: The MS lacks the Bassoon and bass slur, and gives the Horns *fp* instead of *sfp*.

M. 57: The MS lacks the Viola slur to the next measure.

M. 61: The MS lacks the Flute I slur to the next measure, and begins the slur in m. 62 on the first quarter.

Mm. 63/64: In the MS, the Oboe has a slur over both measures.

M. 66: In the MS, the Horns have a whole note (but see m. 70).

M. 68: The First and Second Violin staccato marks are supplied by analogy with m. 72.

M. 69: In the MS, the bass has *f* instead of *sf*.

M. 81: In the MS, the Second Violins have *c#²* (probably only by mistake; in mm. 77–80 the part is not written out, but indicated as "8va bassa").

M. 94: A few staccato marks are supplied here and in mm. 97 and 124.

Mm. 98/99: The MS lacks the Flute I tie.

Mm. 113/114: Here and in mm. 140/141, the MS does not supply the wind slurs consistently, and they have been changed on the basis of the Flute part and mm. 140/141.

Mm. 125/126: The Bassoon slur is supplied by analogy with mm. 98/99.

Mm. 130/131: In the MS, the Bassoon legato mark is only over the 3rd and 4th quarters of m. 130; the alteration here has been made on the basis of mm. 102/103.

Mm. 147/148: The MS lacks the Flute I slur.

Mm. 153/154: The Oboe II legato mark is supplied by analogy with Flute II.

Recitativo

M. 14: Mozart does not indicate "Marcellina" here, but the libretto does. The wording proves conclusively that this passage must be sung by Marcellina and not by Don Curzio, the preceding singer.

No. 18. Sestetto

M. 1: "Andante" was added subsequently. The MS states: "Die Blas-Instrumente auf dem extra Blatt"; their parts are located in the supplement to the MS. The note *f* in the Continuo is in the MS.

Mm. 7/8: The Oboe II legato mark is supplied.

Mm. 16/17: The MS lacks the Oboe II slur.

M. 23: The Oboe slur is supplied.

M. 24: The wind staccato marks are supplied.

M. 25: The MS lacks the First Violin staccato dots here and in m. 27.

M. 45: The MS lacks the Horn I tie to the next measure.

Mm. 50/51: In the MS, the bass has a slur over both measures.

Mm. 64/65: The Viola legato mark is supplied.

M. 67: The bass slur is supplied by analogy with m. 70.

Mm. 78–82: A few staccato dots are supplied.

M. 110: The bass slur is supplied.

M. 138: The MS lacks the slurs in Flutes, Oboes and First and Second Violins.

Recitativo

M. 12: By mistake the MS gives the vocal line the following values: [musical notation]

M. 35: The MS has "♭3" under the *c* of the Continuo.

Mozart has added: "segue l'arietta di Cherubino (dopo l'arietta di Cherubino viene Scena 7ma ch'è un Recitativo istromentato, con aria della Contessa)." This arietta does not occur.

No. 19. Recitativo ed Aria

Mm.	24/25:	The MS lacks the bass legato mark.
Mm.	27/28:	Here and in mm. 29/30, the Oboe and Bassoon slurs are printed as shown in the MS, which is different from the later indications.
M.	33:	The MS lacks the Oboe slurs (also in m. 69).
M.	58:	In the MS, the Bassoons and First Violins have a slur over the whole measure.

Recitativo

Mm.   22ff.:   The original ending in the MS was:

The last two measures are crossed out in red and the new ending, two measures longer, is written beneath in a different hand.

No. 20. Duettino

M.	28:	In the MS, the Bassoons have a slur over the whole measure.
Mm.	31/32:	In the MS, the bass slur is divided by single measures.

No. 21. Coro

Mm.   1/2:   The MS shows the First Violin bowing as:

This has been changed by analogy with the wind parts and mm. 9/10.

M.	11:	In the MS, the Oboe has another *p*.
M.	16:	The bass slur is supplied by analogy with the Viola part.
M.	32:	The MS gives the staccato mark only in the Flute part.

Recitativo

Mm.   17/18:   The MS lacks the rests in m. 17; Mozart proceeds at once, and then writes m. 18 as:

No. 22. Finale

M.	12:	The MS indicates the opening of Scene XIV here, calling it XIII.
M.	19:	The MS lacks the Oboe II slur.
Mm.	20/21:	The MS lacks the Oboe II tie.
M.	41:	The Viola part is printed as in the MS, although it is different from mm. 24, 27 and 38.
Mm.	61ff.:	In the MS, the preceding passage is closed off by a double bar; Mozart begins anew and writes "Scena XIV Coro" over this measure.
M.	62:	The MS lacks the First Violin staccato dots (also in mm. 74 and 82).
M.	63:	The bass staccato dots are supplied.
M.	66:	The MS gives the Violas another *p*.
M.	79:	The MS lacks the First Violin staccato mark (also in mm. 111 and 115).
M.	93:	The bass staccato dots are supplied.
M.	117:	Here, and in m. 206, the *f* for the brass and drums appears on the 1st 8th note.
M.	118:	The MS lacks the Flute II tie to the next measure.
Mm.	134/135:	The MS lacks the First and Second Violin slurs (also in mm. 142/143).
Mm.	137/138:	The bass staccato dots are supplied.
M.	153:	The First and Second Violin staccato dots are supplied.

Mm.	156/157:	The M
M.	168:	The MS la
M.	196:	A few staccato m. 198.
M.	200:	The Flute and First Viol
M.	211:	The MS lacks the Flute II tie

No. 23. Cavatina

M.	14:	The MS lacks the natural sign before the Firs *b*[1].
M.	19:	The MS does not indicate "arco."
M.	22:	The MS lacks the Second Violin staccato marks (in m. 30 they are missing in both violin parts).
M.	27:	The First Violin staccato mark is supplied.
M.	35:	In the MS, the vocal part has a slur between the 1st two notes.
M.	36:	A hand other than Mozart's has crossed out the common-time mark, has added rests (8th-quarter-8th), has entered a *dal segno* mark to apply to m. 10, and has supplied the notes c^2c^2 for the First Violins (see m. 9) and a "Fine" (m. 23).

No. 24. Aria (often omitted in performance, along with the preceding recitative)

M.	11:	The MS lacks the First and Second Violin slur on the 3rd quarter.
M.	25:	The bass staccato dots are supplied (in all the strings in mm. 26, 29 and 30).
Mm.	32/33:	The MS lacks the bass slur to the next measure.
M.	72:	The MS lacks the First and Second Violin staccato dots on the 3rd and 4th quarters.

Recitativo

M.   44:   Mozart has written in: "Dopo l'aria di Basilio viene scena 7ma ch'è un Recitativo Istromentato con aria di Figaro."

No. 25. Aria

M.	7:	The MS lacks the Second Violin staccato dots.
M.	8:	The MS gives the bass another *p*.
Mm.	24/25:	The MS lacks the Bassoon slur.
Mm.	28/29:	The MS lacks the bass slur.
M.	32:	In the MS, the First Violins have a slur over the 3rd and 4th quarters.
M.	38:	The MS lacks the Flute staccato dots and those on the 3rd and 4th quarters of the First and Second Violins (also in m. 40).
Mm.	50/51:	The MS lacks the bass staccato dots.
Mm.	66/67:	In the MS, Clarinet II has a slur (but see the Bassoon part here and in mm. 62/63).
M.	69:	In the MS, the bass has only *sf*.
Mm.	70–74:	In the MS, the wind phrasing differs at times from that in the strings (from the 2nd quarter to the 1st quarter of the next measure).
M.	76:	The MS lacks the bass staccato dots (also in mm. 94/95).
M.	79:	The MS gives the Clarinets a quarter note instead of the 8th note.
Mm.	84/85:	In the MS, the Bassoons have a slur over both measures.
Mm.	91/92:	The MS lacks the bass tie.
M.	121:	The Flute and First Violin slur is supplied by analogy with m. 113.
Mm.	123/124:	In the MS, the bass has a slur over both measures (see mm. 126/127).
Mm.	130/131:	The Bassoon II slur is supplied by analogy with the Clarinet II part.
Mm.	135/136:	The MS lacks the Horn I tie.

No. 26. Recitativo ed Aria (often omitted)

Mm.	1ff.:	The recitative in the MS is not in Mozart's hand.
M.	9:	The MS lacks the *cresc.* and the slur in the Viola part.
M.	11:	The MS gives the Second Violins f^2 (confusion with the Viola part).
M.	15:	The MS lacks the *p*.
M.	24:	In the MS, the winds have an alla-breve signature, the strings common-time.

.ots.
.ne next

of the 3rd
.ne first f^2 of
/S, although

.t measure (also

.ar.
.r p on the 1st quarter.
.s are supplied.
.s and bass sfp, and lacks

No. 27. Rec.

Mm. 12–14: The M.... ....st Violin legato mark.
M. 21: In the MS, the Second Violins lack the slur and the flat sign in front of the b^1.
M. 39: In the MS, the Oboe slur is divided by half measures.
M. 61: The MS lacks the Flute staccato dots.

No. 28. Finale

M. 3: The MS lacks the Oboe I slur (also in m. 36, where it also lacks the Bassoon I slur).
M. 5: The MS gives the bass a slur to the next measure, which does not occur in the other string parts.
Mm. 10/11: The MS lacks the Bassoon II slurs.
Mm. 14–17: The MS notates the First Violin grace notes as 16th notes.
M. 26: The Bassoon II is supplied, as are the Second Violin and Viola staccato marks.
M. 28: The MS lacks the Oboe II slur.
M. 30: The MS places the Second Violin and Viola slur over the 1st–4th 8th notes only, but in m. 31 the 5th 8th note is clearly included in the group.
M. 31: The MS lacks the Second Violin slur.
M. 34: The MS lacks the First and Second Violin staccato dots (also in mm. 35–38; in m. 38, in the Viola part too).
M. 43: The MS marking of the First and Second Violins (which each have a slur over the 3rd and 4th quarters) is obviously incorrect and has been altered by analogy with m. 46. The MS lacks the Bassoon and bass staccato dots. The Viola slur is supplied by analogy with m. 46. In the MS, the Countess' part has a slur from the 1st to the 2nd note.
M. 46: The MS lacks the Bassoon staccato dots.
M. 48: In the MS, Figaro's part has a slur over the first half of the measure.
M. 51: The MS indicates: "Con un po più di motto." The MS lacks the Bassoon and First Violin staccato dots.
M. 67: The MS lacks the Flute II slur.
M. 68: The MS lacks the First Violin staccato dots on the 2nd quarter and those for the Second Violins on the 1st and 2nd quarters.
M. 73: The Viola slur is supplied by analogy with m. 76.

M. 76: In contrast to m. 73, the MS here gives the Second Violins separate slurs over each quarter.
M. 78: In the MS, the slur over the 2nd quarter in the Second Violin part is divided; this is altered here by analogy with m. 75.
M. 87: The MS lacks the Flute I slur. In the MS, the Second Violins have a slur over the whole measure.
M. 89: In the MS, the Second Violin slur is divided by half measures.
M. 92: The MS lacks the Oboe II slur (also in m. 93).
M. 134: Here and in a few later passages, Mozart has extended the First Violin slurs to the next measure.
Mm. 182/183: In the MS, the Clarinet and Bassoon slurs are divided by single measures (see mm. 227/228).
M. 192: The MS lacks the Clarinet ties to the next measure.
Mm. 202/203: The MS lacks the Flute II slur.
M. 205: The Horn II slur to the next measure is supplied by analogy with m. 262.
M. 209: The MS lacks the staccato dots here, but gives them in m. 266.
Mm. 227/228: In the MS, the Second Violin slur is divided by single measures.
M. 229: The MS lacks the Second Violin slur.
Mm. 231/232: In contrast to mm. 182/183 and 227/228, the slurs in the MS are divided by single measures (a slip due to changing lines in the MS).
M. 280: The Viola II slur is supplied.
M. 286: The MS lacks the Flute II slur (also in mm. 306 and 327).
M. 289: The slur indicated in the Flute part is not always notated consistently later for the winds in the MS.
M. 296: The MS lacks the Flute I slur.
Mm. 297–299: In the MS, the Viola and bass staccato marks are shown only in the 2nd half of m. 297.
Mm. 315/316: The Bassoon staccato dots are supplied.
Mm. 317/318: The Flute II slur and Oboe II tie are supplied.
M. 319: The MS places the Bassoon p on the 4th 8th note.
Mm. 335ff.: The MS states: "Die Blas Instrumenten sind auf dem Extra Blatt"; unfortunately, their parts are missing in the MS.
Mm. 343ff.: From here to the end of the opera, the parts of Don Curzio and Bartolo are no longer shown in the MS, presumably because in setting down the opera Mozart knew that only one singer would portray both Basilio and Don Curzio, and one other both Antonio and Bartolo.
Mm. 349/350: The Second Violin and Viola staccato marks are supplied by analogy with the First Violin part.
M. 376: The MS gives the bass only f.
Mm. 379/380: The Oboe II slur is supplied.
M. 380: The MS places the bass f on m. 381.
M. 390: The MS places the Viola f on m. 391 (in m. 392 it is on the 3rd quarter).
M. 395: The bass staccato mark is supplied.
M. 403: The First and Second Violin staccato dots are supplied.
M. 426: The MS lacks the First Violin slur from the 1st to the 2nd quarter.
Mm. 486/487: The basic texts indicate the Oboe I tie here, whereas it is lacking in mm. 496/497 and 506/507.
M. 492: The MS places the f in the women's vocal parts on the 1st quarter of m. 493 (but see m. 502).
M. 503: The MS places the First and Second Violin f on m. 504 (but see m. 493).

Berlin-Wilmersdorf, Summer 1941

GEORG SCHÜNEMANN
KURT SOLDAN